DON'T PUT DAVE IN THE MICROWAVE!

WRITTEN & ILLUSTRATED BY

CHRIS WHITE

CABOODLE BOOKS LTD

First published in Great Britain in 2008 by Caboodle Books Ltd

A Catalogue record for this book is available from the
British Library.

ISBN-13: 978-0-9559711-5-0

Typeset in ITC Century Book by www.envydesign.co.uk

Printed in the UK by CPI Cox & Wyman, Reading

The paper and board used in the paperback by Caboodle Books
Ltd are natural recyclable products made from wood grown in
sustainable forests. The manufacturing processes conform to the
environmental regulations of the country of origin.

Caboodle Books Ltd
Riversdale, 8 Rivock Avenue, Steeton, BD20 6SA
Tel: 01535 656015

CONTENTS

For Reuben...
Love Bish...

PLEASE ALLOW ME TO INTRODUCE MYSELF...

I was born when I was very young.
I don't remember much at all.
I wasn't as large as I am now.
Which was good coz my clothes were
quite small.

But soon I started growing up.
And up and op and op.
I think that's why I'm so tall now,
Coz nobody told me to stop.

My mum looked at me and said "Ooh dear!
Can't I 'av one that's a bit more sweet?!"
But she couldn't take me back to the hospital,
As she'd thrown away the receipt.

So my dear Mum threw me out of the house.
She said life with me was too hard.
I ended up being raised by hedgehogs,
In the bush at the end of our yard.

Soon I trundled off to school,
Where they taught me lots of stuff.
Like you can't go home till 3-15,
Even if you've had enough.
I learnt that 2 plus 2 is 6.
And the capital of France is Milton Keynes.
Sheep can fly, water's dry,
And the currency of Spain is baked beans.

I was going to leave school after 2 weeks,
I knew everything by then it appears!
But I didn't know which one the exit door was,
So I ended up staying ten years…

Then onto earning a living.
I've had some great jobs mind.
Like dry cleaning pigeons, stacking cows,
And training guide tortoises for the blind.

I've travelled the world at least twenty times.
Been everywhere twice I'd have said.
Found myself in many weird places.
But none as weird as inside my head.

Hobbies? You say? Well – I watch the TV.
But I never switch it on.
I like to tickle chickens,
And dress cats up as Pokemon.

One day I wrote and illustrated some poems,
But half way through I got bored.
So don't tell anyone, but the last part
of this book,
Was written by a monkey named Claude.

In the future I'd like to get older.
And maybe sometime soon,
Invent a new flavour Pringle,
And build the first *Little Chef* on the moon.

So that's all you need to know about me,
And what a stroke of luck!
Not only do you get to hear my life story,
You also get to read this book...

DON'T PUT DAVE IN THE MICROWAVE

Mum told my little brother not to
play with his food.
Mum told my little brother, "Try and
be nice and not rude!"
She told him to try and do a good
deed every day,
But there was just one thing that my
Mum forgot to say…

DON'T PUT DAVE IN THE MICROWAVE!

Mum said, "Remember, wash behind your
ears and always brush your hair.
Everyday change your socks and put
on clean underwear!
Go to school and behave yourself –
always pay attention."
But there was one small piece of advice
that my Mum forgot to mention…

DON'T PUT DAVE IN THE MICROWAVE!

Mum said to my little brother,
"Always fold up your clothes."
She told him, "Never, ever eat the stuff
that's up your nose!
Always respect your elders and always
love your mother."
But there was one important thing that
she didn't tell my brother...

DON'T PUT DAVE IN THE MICROWAVE!

Dave was my little pet hamster –
and my brother – not being too clever,
Didn't know that hamsters and microwaves
aren't meant to go together!
How was my brother supposed to know

he was doing a terrible thing?
It still makes me shudder, down my spine,
every time I hear a microwave, "PING!"
Sometimes I wake up in the dead of night, hoping
I was dreaming!
But my sheets are always soaking wet and
I always wake up screaming...

DON'T PUT DAVE IN THE MICROWAVE!

I've got a new hamster called 'Brenda',
these days,
And my brother's not so bad in his ways,
But I think we'll sit down – face to face,
And I'll tell my brother, just in case...

DON'T PUT BRENDA IN THE...

I LEFT MY BRAIN
ON THE TRAIN

I have something I'd like to confess,
And please don't think I'm insane.
You wouldn't believe what I did last week...
I left my brain on the train.

I went to see the train company,
And with a nervous grin,
I asked the man, "Excuse me sir...
Has my brain been handed in?"

We looked in the lost property box
And imagine my relief.
My brain was there - with a teddy bear,
A purse and a pair of false teeth!

But one thing is really bothering me,
And drives me up the wall.
I was walking around with no brain for days,
And no one noticed a difference at all...

MY FRIEND FRED

My friend Fred has a reeeally big head!
And he's got no hair upon it!
If the sun hits it right – it's incredibly bright,
So he has to wear a hat or a bonnet!

My friend Shelly has a reeeeeeally big belly!
It's the largest that I've ever seen!
But she has a use for it – children adore it!
And use her tummy as a trampoline!

My friend Joe's – got a really big nose!
And it has to be admired,
How he uses it for – pigeons galore,
To perch on it when they get tired!

My friend Jade – has no eyes I'm afraid!
Coz something happened that wasn't too neat...
She read so many books from the library,
Her eyes fell out and rolled down the street!

My friend Nash has a massive moustache.
It's been warming his face for years!
As during cold weather – he knits it together
With the hair that grows out of his ears!

My friend Pete has got really big feet!
You should see the size of his shoes!
And if his town floods – guess what he does?
He rents them out as canoes!

13

My friend Clyde – has a huge backside!
It sticks out a mile I'm afraid!
People get shocks – when they see his buttocks!
And his pants are specially made!

THE DROOL POOL

I'm asleep on the sofa
I'm having a dream,
The one about thingy
And the bowl of ice cream...

Then I wake up
And don't think I'm a fool,
But I'm happy to see
A small patch of drool!

It's always a sign
That your sleep has been ace!
A slow trickle of drool
Down the side of your face!

Perhaps you were having
An afternoon nap?
You wake up and it's like
You slept under a tap!

You've had such a snooze!
You slept like a log!
You were so relaxed
You drooled on the dog!

Or maybe at night
You wake up with a grin!
Ooooh what is that moisture
On the end of your chin?

Don't feel embarrassed!
You should feel like a champ!
As you check to see
If your pillow is damp!

If your time asleep
Has been really cool,
You'll have made on your pillow
Your own drool pool!

Can you now see?
How brilliant you've been?
You created that pool
From your own drool stream!

Tell them at work!
Show them in your schools!
Shout it from the roof tops!
All together "DROOL RULES!"

It's warm and it's wet!
Hey – aren't you clever!
But – quick – take a photo,
Coz it won't last forever....

THE PLUG-HOLE HORROR

It's lurking down there…I can hear it…
It's gurgling and swirling and groaning…
As the last of the water drains away
And the bubble bath slowly stops foaming…

IT'S *HAIRY!*   IT'S *SCARY!*
SOUNDS LIKE *MARIAH CAREY!!*

Take a peek down the bath plug-hole…
Look – see that little bit of hair?
It all goes to make a monster,
Who lurks in the dark down there…

IT'S *HAIRY!*   IT'S *SCARY!*
SOUNDS LIKE *MARIAH CAREY!!*

Yes - Every strand of stray hair,
That down the plug-hole disappears,
Be it from Dad's head, or my Mum's legs,
Or from my brother's ears…

Is added to this hairy beast,
'The Plug-Hole Horror' it's called.
One of these days, it'll show its face,
After up the plug-hole it's crawled…

IT'S *HAIRY!*   IT'S *SCARY!*
SOUNDS LIKE *MARIAH CAREY!!*

Beware of this horrendous wail!
It's like nothing you've heard before!
It's a cross between Mariah Carey and a cat,
That's had its tail trapped in a door…

IT'S *HAIRY!*   IT'S *SCARY!*
SOUNDS LIKE *MARIAH CAREY!!*

Yep – 'The Plug- Hole Horror's' terrifying!
The most blood-curdling creature by far!
Scarier than a teacher in a bad mood!
And hairier than my Grandma!

IT'S *HAIRY!*   IT'S *SCARY!*
SOUNDS LIKE *MARIAH CAREY!!*

If you're sitting there soaking –
it may pull you down
The plug-hole in one of its rages!
So, yep – I can't lie – that's the main reason why,
I've not had a bath for aaaages!!.

DÉJÀ VU

Have you ever heard of Déjà vu?
It's when something new is happening to you.
But, it feels like you've done it once before,
Have you or haven't you? – you can't be
too sure…

THE HARE IN A CHAIR

Let me introduce Warren the Hare
Who lives by a hill, near a brook.
Warren has his own wheelchair
As he once got hit by a truck.

Warren has lots of hare friends
That scamper round the fields,
But Warren has trouble following them
Because he's on two wheels.

One day his pals arranged a race
To the top of the hill and back down.
But when Warren wanted to join in too
His friends said, "No," with a frown.

"You wouldn't keep up with us Warren,"
One of the other hares said,
"Why don't you just roll to the finish line
And wait for us there instead."

"Hmmph! Not a chance," mumbled Warren,
"I am going to enter this race.
I'll beat all the other hares over the line!"
A smile on his furry face.

The time of the big race arrived,
"Ready, Steady, GO!"
All the hares shot off like bullets
Except Warren who was a bit slow.

The hasty hares ran up the hill,
The climb for them was nothing.
But miles behind came Warren in his chair,
Sweating, panting, puffing!

As everyone else sped over the hill
Warren heard one hare say,
"We'll have to come back and get Warren,
To get up here will take him all day!"

"I'll show them!" Warren shouted
And gripped his wheels tight.
His arms, his paws, his body, his mind,
Pumped with all his might.

On the downward path to the finish line,
The hares were racing still.
But look! Who's that in the distance,
Just on the brow of the hill?!

He's moving like a torpedo!
This race will go to the wire!
He's overtaking everyone!
It's Warren in his chair-iot of fire!

The wheelchair hare was a blur!
As towards the line he came pelting!
His eyes rolling in their sockets!
His tyres nearly melting!

His white hot wheelchair shot past the others
Scaring some half to death!
And he pipped them all to the winning post
Not by much – just a hair's breadth!

As his friends all gasped, Warren yelled,
"Don't judge me by my appearance!
It's amazing what a hare can do
With grit and perseverance."

The hares all hugged Warren warmly,
And lifted him up in the air.
"Three chairs for Warren!" They shouted,
"The heroic hare in a chair!!"

PIRATE DENTIST

I go to this pirate dentist.
He's the best around by far!
You sit in the chair – stick your tongue in the air,
Open your mouth and say…

BACKWARDS WENT
IT DAY THE

Some days are really strange,
And things just go a bit wrong.
Like the day everything went backwards.
Let me tell you what went on…

I woke up just like usual,
And went to have a shower – like you do.
But instead of getting cleaner,
I got dirtier and smellier too.

Then a quick whip round with the toothbrush,
But I thought "I'm going mad!
My teeth are getting more yellow
And my breath smells really bad!"

So I went to my bedroom to try and get dressed,
But I really wasn't too sure,
How I ended up in my pants and socks,
And my clothes folded up in the drawer.

Then I went to play football with my mates,
And things were fine until,
The ref blew for full time before we'd kicked off,
And we went from 3-2 to 0-0!

MMm! Then it was time for dinner,
But it really wasn't that great,
To see food come rushing out of my mouth
And appear freshly cooked on my plate!

So I went home and thought
"I'll read a book for a bit.
When I've finished, this madness might've gone!"
I started the book on page 103,
And finished it on page one…

I got ready for bed – but I needed the loo…
AND GOOD GRIEF! THE FRUSTRATION!!
But there are something's I'd rather
not talk about,
So I'll leave that to your imagination…

I lay in bed staring out of the window,
Trying to work out what was happening, and why.
As I watched puddles turning into rain,
And shoot up into the sky.

"At least this backward day's
nearly over!" I thought,
As I slowly drifted away.
But imagine my surprise when
I woke in the morning,
And found it was yesterday!

THE FREAKY FARM

Welcome to the Freaky Farm,
Don't worry – there's nothing to fear!
But you may see a few strange creatures,
Wandering around in here…

Take for example – this weird animal…
It's called a 'Crococow,'
Part farmyard beast – part reptile.
(I know – don't ask me how!)

She's black and white and scaly.
Has hooves and a long tail too.
There are rows of sharp teeth in
her mighty mouth,
Which she sometimes opens to 'Moooo!'

Apparently her milk is delicious!
From her udder – pink and soft.
Though the last person who tried to milk her,
Had both of his arms bitten off!

GOONJO

Wow! It's a very rare 'Goonjo!'
A bird written of in folklore!
Look – it's half goose and half banjo!
I've never seen one before!

She'll open her beak and make twangy sounds.
This one looks in perfect health!
So if we're lucky we may just see,
This creature pluck itself!

OCTOSHEEP

Wow! That's an Octosheep over there,
A thing born of an Octopus and a Sheep!
He has eight legs – bleats a lot,
And dives in a pond to sleep.

Pop a knitting needle on each of its legs,
And you couldn't wish for much better!
His fleece is so full – he'll use his own wool,
To knit you up a quick sweater!

DRICKEN

Look! There is a Dricken!
Half Dragon – half farmyard bird!
She has two wings – is covered with feathers,
And really looks absurd!

But the good thing about a Dricken,
Is not her horns or scrawny legs,
But when she breathes fire from her beak,
She'll sometimes poach her own eggs!

THE LIFE OF STOOART STOOPID

The life of Stooart Stoopid
Was a short and stoopid one.
He did many, many stoopid things,
But was too thick to know what he'd done.

As a baby – Stooart showed early signs
Of how stoopid he would become.
He would often suck a nappy
And stick a dummy up his bum.

Whilst a toddler – he'd visit the
park with his mum.
But Stooart would get out of hand.
He would make little castles in the duck pond
And try to feed bread to the sand…

Stooart's years at school weren't much better.
His results weren't the cream of the crop.
If he took an exam – he would take the two hours,
Just writing his name at the top.

Stooart's parents thought he'd like some pets.
"It might do him good!" they agreed.
Except Stooart squeezed his dog in a bowl,
And dragged his fish round the streets on a lead.

Out he went to find his first job,
Which was a paper round.
But stoopid Stooart couldn't deliver them,
Because of the problem he found.

"I can't get the papers through the letter boxes!
They're too long and wide!" he would roar.
Stooart never thought of rolling them up
To fit them through the door!

Stooart found his very first girlfriend!
And wanted to give her a snog!
They smooched in the dark – then on
came the lights,
And he'd been French kissing her dog!

One day Stooart helped with the ironing.
Then the phone rang and … oh dear!
Stooart got very very confused,
And ended up burning his ear!

At Xmas time Stooart cooked dinner!
And what did he get right – nuffing!
He sat stroking the frozen turkey on his lap,
And he gave the cat a good stuffing!

I'm afraid Stooart Stoopid died last year,
In the prime of his stoopid life.
He left behind one stoopid baby,
And Stacey – his stoopid wife.

Stooart's funeral was a lovely occasion.
It was perfect – except in one way.
Stooart was stoopid – right to the end,
And forgot to turn up on the day!

WILLIE THE WILD WEST WASP

Women and children hid in fear.
Even cowboys wore a frown,
When Willie the Wild West Wasp,
Decided to fly into town.

He terrorised the whole neighbourhood,
He made the locals scream!
He buzzed around the heads
Of anyone with an ice cream.

Willie has six little arms
Around which six guns are slung.
No one dare touch him or they would find out
How the West was stung!

Then suddenly in the distance,
Coming this way in full flight,
Is Deputy Daddy Long Legs,
Looking for a fight!

There they both hovered in the High Street,
Ready for a Wild West brawl!
The local undertaker measured them up
For two coffins – about an inch tall…

The two insects eyed each other up,
In front of the gathering throng.
Willie wondered where the deputy
bought his chaps,
Coz his legs were reeeeeaaaally long!

Then as the tension mounted,
One of the crowd shouted "DRAW!!"
12 shots rang out and both insects,
Lay on their backs on the floor.

Were they such great shots that
they'd killed one another?
Had they both cruelly ended this caper?
Nope – the local Sheriff had thought
"ENOUGH OF THIS RUBBISH!"
And swotted them both with his paper!!

49

PIGS MIGHT FLY

Aaah! Just imagine if hedgehogs could fly!
They would be happy days.
No more scraping flat hedgehogs off,
Our dual carriageways!

Oooh! Just think if elephants could fly,
That'd be great I bet!
We could all jump aboard – fly on holiday,
And call it a Jumbo Jet!

How about if cows could fly above?!
And you were in the wrong place,
Then with a splat! A smelly cow pat,
hits you right in the face!

If cats could fly – what fun we'd have!
No one would be bored – you see,
We could grip 'em whilst curled up and sleeping,
Then use them as a Frisbee!

If tortoises could fly – now that would be bad.
And let me tell you why,
We'd all have to wear crash helmets,
In case they fell out of the sky!!

Hey – just imagine if monkeys could fly!
Now – that would be all right!
We could tie some string round their tail,
And fly 'em like a kite!

And just think if I was a millionaire,
And mansions and yachts I could buy!
All because I'd sold loads and loads of books…
Yeh – and pigs might fly…

51

IN THE PARK

I went to the park.
With my dog and his ball.
We were throwing and catching.
No worries at all.

But then I was thinking.
About the ball we were throwing.
From me to my dog.
To-ing and fro-ing.

I couldn't work out.
No – I just couldn't figure.
Why, when the ball came towards me.
It looked a lot bigger…

…and then it hit me.

VICKY THE SLIGHTLY LESS THAN AVERAGE LOOKING DUCKLING

There was once a little duckling called Vicky,
Who wasn't one of the ugly ducks,
But as we have to be politically correct,
She had slightly less than average looks.

But there was nothing really wrong with her.
All the other ducks said that – but still,
This duck thought she was a bit chubby,
With a slightly wonky bill.

"All the other ducks look perfect," she sobbed,
As some bread was thrown into the lake.
Vicky ignored it as the others tucked in.
(She'd had today's calorie intake.)

Vicky wanted to be someone.
Maybe get on TV.
But she thought it would never happen because,
She thought she looked too freaky.

Later that evening the ducks noticed,
A note pinned to the tree.
It was addressed 'To All the Perfect Ducks...'
And signed, 'From Vile Vicky.'

'Dear Friends,' it said – one clever duck read,
'Please don't worry for me.
But I'm booked into a clinic tonight,
For plastic surgery.'

The ducks all looked at each other.
Some looked worried – some thought it funny.
A couple looked at each other and quacked,
"Where did she get all the money?"

Vicky returned after a week,
With a completely brand new look.
"What a transformation!" they cried,
"You look like a different duck!"

Her bill was straight and smaller.
Feathers dyed, not dull like before.
She'd been sucked and tucked, nipped and pinned,
She even didn't have webbed feet anymore!

All the other ducks rushed towards her,
Wanting to prod and touch!
Vicky wanted to quack with delight,
But her bill was hurting too much!

A few days later – what should come along,
But a nature documentary crew.
They wanted to film ducks in the wild,
So their viewers could see what they do.

57

"This is my big chance!" Vicky thought,
  "I'm gonna be a big star you know!
I look so perfect – how can they resist,
  Making me the star of the show?"

The director yelled "This documentary's about,
  Natural ducks doing natural things.
With your ruffled feathers, wonky bills,
  Webbed feet and battered wings!"

"Get rid of that rubber duck over there!
  It looks wrong for goodness sake!
We're only filming natural, beautiful ducks,
  Not ones that are plastic and fake!"

The other ducks were a huge success,
  And had long TV careers.
Vicky the Duck was right out of luck,
  Left all alone and in tears.

There's a lesson in here somewhere.
Be who you are – that's what matters.
Just be yourself – not like Vicky,
  Absolutely quackers.

I KNOW A FLY THAT SWALLOWED AN OLD LADY

I know a fly that swallowed an old lady,
"I didn't mean to!" he said," She sort
of just made me!
She kept trying to swat me, yelling 'DIE! DIE!'
You'd think she'd never seen a six foot fly!"

"So I swallowed a cat," continued the fly,
"If you 'ang on a sec, I'll tell ya why.
I thought it might be company for 'er.
How was I to know she's allergic to fur?!"

"So I swallowed a vet – to put down the cat.
A quick jab, I thought, and that'll be that!
But the vet's bill was huge – well beyond a joke,
And ya know, at the mo, I'm a little bit broke."

"So I swallowed a hit man to take care of the vet.
(By this time I was severely in debt.)
As I gave a few quid to this man from the mob,
And the rest would be due on completion
of the job…"

"But – I wasn't to know – don't think me a fool,
The lady, hit man and vet went to
the same school!
'Let's catch up – I've missed ya!'
Each person confesses,
They exchange phone numbers
and e-mail addresses!"

"THIS IS GETTING' STUPID!! I scream –
nearly cryin',
So I go and swallow a man eatin' lion!
That'll get 'em, I thought, but as time passes,
I realise the lady's had lion tamin' classes!"

"And don't ask me how she found 'em in there,
But she tamed that lion with a whip and a chair!
I just don't believe it – I'm full of dismay!
This fly is havin' one really bad day!"

"What are the chances of all this happenin'?"
(The fly's stomach starts groaning and gurgling)
"Now I wish that lady," the fly did confess,
"Had swotted me first with 'er Daily Express."

"Swallowing that biddy was one big mistake!
And it's given this fly one big belly ache!
It has to be said, and I'm sure you'll agree,
The things I've eaten don't agree with me!"

I know two Rennies that were swallowed by a fly.
'Plop! Plop! Fizz! Gurgle!' It was worth a try…
Did that fly recover? Don't make that suggestion.
I know an old fly who died from indigestion…

PETER ANTEATER

Peter Anteater had problems in the winter.
When things get cold and not nice.
He couldn't eat any ants at all,
As the insects were covered in ice.

But his friend (Wayne the Anteater)
Said "Peter, would you please,
Take a can of this – it works a treat!"
What was it? Anty Freeze!

THE GENIE
OF THE KETTLE

So, I was in the kitchen the other day,
And imagine my surprise,
When I switched on the kettle, smoke came out…
And something appeared in front of my eyes…

Yes! It was amazing!
It was only this big – quite teeny,
But there floated a magic spirit,
Who said, "Hi! I'm a Kettle Genie!"

"A what?" I asked "A Kettle Genie!" he said,
"You've unleashed me for goodness sake!
And now I am your lifelong slave…
So one wish you can make!"

"One wish?!" I said, "That's a bit naff!
I thought you're supposed to grant three?"
"Nah!" he mumbled, "That's the big boys…
I'm just a small Kettle Genie…"

So I started thinking, "Ooooh! What shall I wish for?
A mansion with acres of grounds?
Unlimited chocolate? A monkey that talks?
Or a billion squillion pounds?!"

"Err!" I should warn you…" The Genie butted in,
"Yeh – I really think I oughta.
You see the only magic power I have,
Is the ability to boil water…"

"WHAAATT!!" I blurted "That's rubbish!!
Who would wish for that? Are you dim?"
But the Genie started crying a bit,
So I felt a bit sorry for him.

So he granted my wish and the water boiled,
Then the Kettle Genie disappeared
And as I sat sipping my cup of tea,
I thought "Hmmm! Now that was just weird…"

68

LOSING FACE

One morning, I woke up and I'd lost my face!
I immediately started fretting!
No eyes, no ears – my mouth disappeared!
It really was quite upsetting!

I'm sure I had it when I went to sleep.
It must have fallen off in the night!
How am I supposed to do things now?
This really is not right!

I'll never smell fresh cut grass again!
No more hearing music for me!
The taste of chocolate pud, is gone for good!
And sunsets I'll no longer see!

Sure, my face wasn't perfect.
My nose was big – ears stuck out a bit.
But I really want my face back.
My head's naked without it!

It wasn't the most beautiful face,
Like you see on TV.
But that doesn't seem important now.
That face was the face of me!

Perhaps it slipped under my pillow.
Or my face is face down on the floor.
I promise, if I find it, I'll never, ever, ever,
Take my face on face value anymore!

UNICORN

"Oh just what is the point of me?"
The unicorn shouted out loud.
"If you put me in a field of horses,
I stick right out from the crowd."

"Why – oh – why is this horn on my head?
It just looks stupid and naff!
If I had two, it would look pretty cool,
But just one? You're having a laugh!"

"I'll never be able to wear a hat
Or even a helmet or bonnet!
And I'm afraid I always skewer,
Any bird that perches on it!"

As the unicorn took a stroll down the street,
Bemoaning her looks and her plans,
She was startled by all the litter around,
The crisp packets, chip wrappers and cans...

The unicorn had an idea that day,
And no longer is twisted and bitter!
You won't see her mourn – she now uses her horn,
To pick up any stray bits of litter!

ONE MAN AND HIS DOG

An old shepherd sent his dog out
to fetch his sheep in,
(There were 36 – scattered over the moors.)
Darting this way and that, with a woof and a bark!
The dog scampered round on his paws.

The shepherd whistled the dog
and sheep back to him,
"Do we have them all in, my old pup?"
"Yep – all 40" he barked - The shepherd
quizzed "Not 36?"
"Oh Sorry! I was rounding them up…"

SANTA

Santa works on Christmas Eve,
Delivering gifts far and near.
But what on earth does Santa do
For the rest of the year?

Does he run a pizza takeaway?
Making pizza that everyone likes?
If you live within 5 miles – it's delivered
hot and fresh,
By elves on motor-bikes?

Or does he rescue small children from mineshafts,
Who have had a terrible fall?
If he squeezes down chimneys on Christmas Eve,
That shouldn't be a problem at all!

Perhaps he drives round council estates,
On a really hot summer's day?
Selling ice-creams and choc ices,
From the back of his magical sleigh!

Or…Does he take his reindeers to Blackpool
And fit them with a saddle each…
Then charge three pounds fifty to take little kids
On a ride up and down the beach?

I think that we should try and find out
What Santa does all year!
But not now – there's a knock at my front door…
I think my pizza's here…….

CAPTAIN COD: UNDERWATER SQUAD

Has crime been committed under the sea?
Have somebody's valuables gone?
Call Captain Cod: Underwater Squad,
For fishy goings on.

He's the best detective in the ocean.
The most cunning cod you ever saw!
No fishy felons can escape,
The long fin of the law!

Take the time the ocean bank was robbed,
Who did it? There weren't any hints!
But Captain Cod saved the day,
By dusting for fish-finger prints.

And there was once a riot on the sea bed,
But in a stunning show of fish force,
Captain Cod rounded up the hooligans,
On the back of a police sea horse.

Yes – Captain Cod is in perfect shape,
And his brain is razor sharp.
Most criminals when the plan is foiled,
Admit, "It's a fair carp."

Our officer of the ocean is always prepared.
He even carries four pairs of handcuffs.
Just in case he has to arrest,
A drunken octopus.

The sea bed is calm and peaceful thanks to him.
It's a much safer place to go,
He got rid of the troublesome sea urchins,
By slapping them with an ASBO.

From cat fish burglars to lobsters pinching,
Our scaly hero will be there!
Seeking the truth – avoiding red herrings,
So the slippery scales of justice are fair!

A crab stick up or a hit and swim,
You know who'll show his fish face!
Yes – criminal fish have had their chips!
Captain Cod is on the case!!

DÉJÀ VU

Have you ever heard of Déjà vu?
It's when something new is happening to you.
But, it feels like you've done it once before,
Have you or haven't you? – you can't
be too sure…

THE HUGE HAIRY PIG

I went to a party the other day.
The room it was in was so big!
It was full of interesting people to meet
And I got talking to a huge hairy pig.

This pig talked about his family,
His travels, his sty, his job.
He talked and talked for ages.
This pig would not shut his gob!

On and on and on he went.
On and on and on…
On and on and on and on,
On and on and on…

And on and on and on and on,
On and on and on.
On and on and on and on,
On and on and on.

Then on and on and on and on.
On and on and on.
On and on and on and on.
On and on and on.

After what seemed like hours,
I just couldn't take anymore!
It turns out he wasn't a huge hairy pig,
Just a great big hairy boar!

SIMON THE WORKER ANT

Here's a poem, here we go,
About an ant that we all know.
Simon the ant – it's no surprise,
Has six skinny legs and two bug eyes.

All Simon does is work and work,
Day after day – no time to shirk.
Moving rocks and dirt from here to there,
Simon thinks this isn't fair!

Simon's part of a colony,
Thousands of ants – a big family.
And every ant – whatever their name,
Looks pretty much the same.

"I'm so bored" Simon would complain,
"All this work drives me insane!
Every day and every one,
Is so dull - where is the fun?"

So Simon had a super plan,
"I'm gonna change things if I can!"
He tiptoed round in the middle of the night,
Lots of ideas burning bright.

Simon has a huge passion.
He always wanted to work in fashion!
He'd designed a range of stunning clothes,
For all the ants that he knows!

So the next day at work, it wasn't dull!
It was an ant carnival!
The ants dressed up from head to toe,
Looking faaaaaboulous darling – Dontcha know?

Thanks to Simon all the ants,
Wore bright red shirts and orange pants!
Yellow hats, and who would think?
Three pairs of socks in fuchsia pink!

Thanks to Simon's great designs,
All the ants now have good times!
They do their work at a greater pace,
With a great big smile on their face!

And Simon the ant went on to be,
The greatest designer in history!
You'll see his clothes – if you can,
In London, Paris and Milan!

Simon rose above the other ants,
He now lives in the south of France.
You won't find him moving dirt and rocks,
You'll find him on his luxury yachts!

DUUUUDE IT'S DIRK THE DINOSAUR

Wooooah! Look – it's daredevil Dirk,
The heroic dinosaur.
No challenge is too rough – no danger too great!
Hear his manly 'ROOOOOAAAAARRRRR!'

Nothing scares him – he's extreme to the max!
He's a rock-climbing, snow-boarding duuuude!
He'll bungee jump, skateboard, cycle and surf,
And he sometimes swims in the nude.

Dirk always wears the latest threads,
His hair style is well fierce.
He's got tattoos on his tattoos,
And has his tail pierced.

Yeaaah! Nothing can hold Dirk Dinosaur back!
He's unstoppable - no doubt!
Oh – until a meteorite hit the earth,
And wiped all the dinosaurs out...

MY TEACHER:
MR D. RAKOOLA

I know most teachers are very strange,
But my teacher is stranger than most.
He's got two fangs, wears a long cloak
And looks as pale as a ghost.

If you were in my class at school,
You'd see he's a weird lookin' fella.
I've heard he doesn't go home at half three,
But sleeps in a crypt in the cellar.

The blinds in our classroom are always closed,
Even when it's a sunny day!
And when I sit down for the register
He looks at my neck in a funny way.

I've never seen him eat a school dinner.
On raw meat he is fed!
And he doesn't drink tea like the other teachers,
In his mug is a liquid that's red!

Lessons are funny with my teacher too,
We don't write stories or poems that rhyme,
Maths we don't need, coz all we do is read,
Bram Stoker all the time!

If you sneak back to school when it gets dark
And really keep your eyes peeled,
I've heard a rumour you can sometimes see him,
Flying over the playing field!

We've got show and tell tomorrow.
What objects will I show with pride?
I'm gonna bring in a crucifix and garlic
Just to be on the safe side.

DBP

See the duck billed platypus.
See her as she plays.
See her stop to cross the road.
See her not look both ways.

See the bus coming quickly.
See the shock of the platypus.
See the tyre marks on the road.
See the duck billed flatypus.

I BOUGHT THIS WHALE AT A CAR BOOT SALE

It was a sunny Sunday morning,
In bed I wanted to lie.
But now I'm glad I went with my Dad,
And let me tell you why…

I BOUGHT THIS WHALE AT A CAR BOOT SALE!
I couldn't believe my eyes!
I BOUGHT THIS WHALE AT A CAR BOOT SALE!
Imagine my surprise!

Just looking round the different stalls,
A faded lampshade – broken pen,
A china pig – someone's old wig,
Nothing exciting… but then…

I BOUGHT THIS WHALE AT A CAR BOOT SALE!
This really pleases me!
I BOUGHT THIS WHALE AT A CAR BOOT SALE!
It was only 50p!

What was the whale doing there?
How could he survive on dry land?
I hurried to pay, coz it's not everyday,
You see a whale for sale – second hand...

I BOUGHT THIS WHALE AT A CAR BOOT SALE!
It's really made my day!
I BOUGHT THIS WHALE AT A CAR BOOT SALE!
It's amazing what folks throw away!

All my friends can't believe I've got him,
My massive mammal mate!
When they ask where I got him from,
I tell it to them straight...

I BOUGHT THIS WHALE AT A CAR BOOT SALE!
It really is unique!
I BOUGHT THIS WHALE AT A CAR BOOT SALE!
I wonder what I'll pick up next week?

BABOON BUBBLEGUM BUM

A normal baboon – that's what he was.
But that was years ago.
Now he's a little bit different,
This is how it came to be so...

This baboon had a hairy bottom,
As all baboons once had.
But things were about to change for good,
But the changing for good, was quite bad.

It was a day like any other,
For our lovely hairy baboon.
He was going to the cinema,
One rainy afternoon.

He loved to watch films with his friends in,
'Planet of the Apes', 'Outbreak',
That day he was watching King Kong ,
even though,
He'd seen it ten times that week for chimp's sake!

He paid his money – sat in his seat,
Ate his popcorn – watched the show,
He was quite happy, but things went quite wrong,
As Baboon stood up to go…

There was some bubblegum on his seat,
And the damage had been done!
As Baboon got up with a massive
"RRRRRIIPPPPPP!!"
And the fur was torn from his bum!

What a rage that put him in!
And he's been in a mood to this day!
As people laugh and point and snigger,
At his bald red cheeks on display!

And baboons are like that to this very day.

They scream and howl and shout!

But today we've got to the bottom of it!

It's because their bottoms hang out!

TIGER FEET

Jermain the tiger was bored one day.
"I need a hobby!" he said, scratching his belly.
"Something to get me out of the house,
And away from watching the telly…"

Now, Jermain had rhythm in his paws
He's quite a mover – so they say!
"Perhaps I should join a dancing class!
Maybe tap, ballroom or ballet?!"

So the very next evening Jermain headed for,
His local community centre.
There were loads of rooms there – with different
classes inside,
But which one should he enter…?

Jermain's mind was then made up,
As he peered into one of the rooms!
The dancers inside were in rows and all moving
To country and western tunes!

But the instructor wouldn't let Jermain join
And they nearly got into a fight!
The tiger had to go – he wasn't to know,
That Tuesday was Lion Dancing night!!

MARGARET THE MERMAID

Margaret isn't like other girls,
For starters – she is half a fish!
But to blend in with her human pals,
Has always been her wish.

When she goes round to her friends' houses,
They still chat and gossip and laugh,
Her friends just lie on the bed or settee,
While Margaret reclines in the bath!

But when all of her buddies go shopping,
Margaret will be there – no doubt!
It's just when they go into shoe shops,
That she feels a little left out.

But – every sports day at the swimming baths –
she's brill!
That's when Margaret's really in the swim.
She's at the finishing line and is holding the cup,
Before anyone else has dived in!

DISCO PIG

The lights are flashing all around.
The beat is getting hot!
Everyone gets on the dance floor,
To show you what they've got!

Some people wiggle like this…
Some people do a jig…
But you ain't ever seen dancing,
'Til you've seen the Disco Pig!

Disco Pig is one cool swine!
He's funky without fail!
He's hip you know, from his afro,
To the tip of his curly tail.

He wears his funky medallion,
Pure gold – if you've not guessed.
And he's the only pig I've seen,
Who has a hairy chest!

The girls all love Disco Pig,
They think he is a cutey!
Yeah – no one can resist it when,
He shakes his piggy booty!

His trotters will just be a blur,
Disco Pig never stops.
Like John Travolta with a snout,
He'll sizzle like pork chops!

Yes – The Disco Pig's perfection,
Buff body – winning smile.
This ain't no pot-bellied pig,
He puts the sty in style!

Though, during the day, he's like normal pigs,
Just chillin' round the farm.
But at night he's alive to The Jackson Five,
Abba or Chaka Khan…Chaka Khan…
Chaka Khan…

So next time you're out dancing,
Better hold onto your wig!
That little pink dude, who's in the groove,
Will be the Disco Pig!!

WALTER THE OVERWEIGHT WEASEL

Walter was a weasel.
He was vewy overweight.
The weason Walter was weighty,
Was that he ate and ate.

Walter was weally widiculous,
When it came to eating food.
He'd shovel anything into his mouth,
And his manners were weally wude.

Wice or wasberries or woast beef,
Waffles, wine gums, waisins or wabbit,
Wheat Cwunchies, wadish or wavioli,
Walter the weasel would have it!

But eating that way is a wotten idea.
You should see how much Walter weighed!
One day – his tummy could take no more…
And pop went the weasel I'm afwaid!

THERE'S SOMTHIN' IN THE DUSTBIN

There's somethin' in the dustbin!
Oh what could it be?
I just started to take the rubbish out,
And it was in there winking at me!

There's somethin' in the dustbin!
I think I'd better beware!
It's making gurgling noises
And moving round in there!

There's somethin' in the dustbin!
Perhaps I should retreat?
I just got a whiff of whatever it is,
And it smells a bit like feet!!

There's somethin' in the dustbin!
What sort of thing would lay,
On top of potato peelings, old cheese
And last night's Chinese take-away?

There's somethin' in the dustbin!
What is lurking inside?
I think I should just put the lid back on
And go back in the house and hide……..

FRIDGE FAIRIES

Think of all the different food,
Your fridge contains right now.
Maybe stinky cheese from a goat,
Perhaps milk from a cow.

As well as meat and a dozen eggs
And yoghurt from local dairies.
Did you know – in there as well,
Could be a few Fridge Fairies?

They're only teeny tiny.
They wear scarves, hats and thick socks.
You may just see, two or three
Asleep in the salad box.

If you ever get to ask one,
She'll say "I'm a sunshine hater!"
They love to be cold and that's why they live,
In your refrigerator!

Our fairy friends are no trouble at all,
Just round the shelves they'll flutter.
Occasionally they'll nibble your coleslaw,
Or leave tiny footprints in the butter.

But the most important job they do,
(If you didn't know before)
Is switching on the little light,
Whenever you open the door.

So watch out for their rosy faces,
They could be there this minute!
Put down this book – to the fridge – take a look!
There could be a Fridge Fairy in it!

LISA

Lisa Lobster was doing some D.I.Y,
And trying to build a shed.
It was somewhere to put her l
awnmower and spade,
So they weren't lying round the sea bed.

But Lisa was struggling a little.
She had plenty of nails, like she should,
But couldn't put her claws on anything,
To bang them into the wood.

But she needn't have worried –
her shed is now done,
Thanks to her good neighbour, Mark.
That's one of the many advantages of,
Living next to a hammer-head shark!

THE MYSTERIOUS
MR PIGGLES

Someone new has moved next door,
And he looks a little bit funny.
I saw him in the back garden,
Rubbing mud on his tummy.

I can't quite put my finger on it,
It's just a weird feeling,
But is it right, in the dead of night,
To be woken by snuffling and squealing?

I saw him go to the shops today,
And the wind blew off his hat.
Two pink floppy ears hung from his head.
Now what do you think of that?

I noticed him fetching his bin in,
(I'd happened to wake up early)
And I'm sure from the back of his jim-jams,
Peeked a tail – pink and curly!

I invited my neighbour round for tea.
I would get to know him at last!
But when I served him a bacon sandwich,
I never saw him run so fast!!

I really must get to the bottom of this!
What makes my neighbour so weird?
I wish I could find a clue or two,
But none have ever appeared.

I managed to find out his name yesterday,
Because a letter came,
It was sent to my house by mistake,
'Mr Piggles' is his name...

"I know!" I thought, "I'll take it round,
And pop it through his door.
Maybe I'll peek in his letter box,
To try and discover more...

Well – I posted his letter – then peered in his home,
Then let out a disgusted cry!
I don't know who the 'Mysterious Mr Piggles' is,
But his house sure is a pig-sty!

GUS THE GHOST

I've got a ghost in my house.
But, to be honest, he's not the best.
I wish I could boast – but he's a rubbish ghost,
Not as scary as the rest.

I wish I had a better one,
I've given this one a chance,
But he's not very good – doesn't frighten
like he should,

He's just a little bit pants.
Take for example, what he did,
Just the other day.
Some friends came round and a ghost that is sound,
Is supposed to scare people away.

But instead of being menacing and evil,
So everyone would flee,
He invited them in, with a wave and a grin,
And made a nice pot of tea.

You would think that Gus might wreck the house.
Throwing tables and chairs in a fluster!
But he'll not rattle your bed – he tidies up instead!
Then has a whip round with a duster!

Most ghosts should shriek and wail and groan!
For hour after hour.
The only wailing you'll hear, when this ghost is near,
Is when he sings in the shower.

You may have heard stories of ghosts that will,
Appear to give you a scare!
They fly round the room, bringing evil and doom,
And leave a foul stench in the air…

But Gus is nothing like that.
Foul stenches? No - he won't leave one!
Except the odd day, he gets carried away,
And puts too much aftershave on!

When the lights go down, a decent ghost,
Will make noises all night through.
You can't sleep tonight – you're trembling
with fright!
There's a cackle! A thud! A Wooooooh!!

My ghost just occasionally makes
a noise in the night,
And I'm embarrassed to tell you of it.
I wish he would learn – I have to tell him to turn,
His Celine Dion tapes down a bit.

So there he is – Gus the Ghost.

The lamest spirit in history.

If you have a ghost too – I've a question for you…

Would anyone please swap with me??

HANG ON...I'VE GOT A QUESTION

Does anyone know,
Anyone at all,
If a 'fly' can't fly,
Do you call it a 'crawl'??

I've not flown
since the 60's...

Aaah...
Those were
the days...

THE WOOLLY MAMMOTH

I know what you're thinking! I can read your mind!
I can tell what you're wondering – no doubt!
It's…"I wonder how exactly did,
Woolly Mammoths die out?"

Well, let me tell you how it went down.
You'll learn something – don't worry – it's not dull!
For it's a little known fact that Woolly Mammoths,
Were actually made of wool.

When God was bored one wet Sunday,
And there was nothing on TV,
He picked up his knitting needles
And a ball of wool or three.

The Lord knitted one – then pearled one,
He didn't need a pattern or nothing.
And when The Almighty had finished his work,
He filled that mammoth with stuffing.

Neither Ice Age nor meteorites
killed them off – Oh no!
That's just rumours and lies!
So how do you explain archaeologists
finding buttons
That God had used for their eyes?

Well, the reason these woolly beasts are all gone,
Is very simple indeed,
And you'll find that out in a second,
As there's just one more verse to read.

The mammoths plodded round
the prehistoric world,
All over the place they travelled,
But they'd snag themselves on branches and rocks.
And Woolly Mammoths… just…unravelled…

FLY KILLER

My friend is doing exams at the mo,
As when he grows up he wants to be,
A top professional fly killer!
So he must pass all his tests you see.

He's been locked in his room revising for weeks.
You can hear him thinking and plotting.
Who'd have thought that to be a fly killer,
You'd have to do so much swotting?

LIBRARY BOOK

I went to my local library,
To borrow a book or two.
After many hours deciding,
I picked one up covered in glue.

The librarian stamped my borrowed book,
And I ran home with great haste.
I couldn't wait to get stuck in,
To my brand new book of paste!

I lay on my bed and began to read,
"Hope it's good!" I thought with a frown.
But I needn't have worried – after a while,
I couldn't put it down!

PIRANHAS IN PYJAMAS

Piranhas in Pyjamas are sat on my settee.
I came downstairs and there they were –
sat watching TV.
They're laughing at the cartoons,
whilst cuddling their teddies.
One's got a plate of jam on toast –
one a bowl of Shreddies.

What time did they get up? How long
have they been here?
They look quite happy and relaxed.
Should I go up to one and shake his fin?
What happens if he flips and attacks?

It's probably best if I leave them be,
I don't want to make them stressed.
They've got to move soon, as sometime
before noon,
They'll surely have to go and get dressed.

I don't really want them to bite my face
Or start chewing my head!
So I think I'll forget watching TV,
And go read a book instead.

MR CRANKY PANTS

I've a friend who's never happy.
He shouts! He raves! He rants!
He's the most miserable man for miles.
He's Mr Cranky Pants.

I've never heard him laugh,
Not even by mistake.
If he ever cracked a smile,
His face would probably break!

If it is a sunny day,
He'll say "It's too hot for me!"
But if it's cold, he'll still complain,
"Does it have to be so chilly?"

Yep – he's never, ever satisfied.
He's just a grumpy goon.
His lip sticks out – his forehead frowns.
A face just like a prune.

He doesn't like dancing – he doesn't like singing,
For ice cream he does not care!
He doesn't like books – he doesn't like sport,
He really is a nightmare!

There are one or two things he does like though.
He likes covering a pound coin with glue,
Sticking it to the pavement – then watching folks,
Try to pick it up for an hour or two.

Or he loves giving babies really big balloons,
So they float up into the sky!
Then he'll sit on a bench in the park all day,
And watch babies drifting by......

Or he'll nip to the zoo and put hair dye,
In the water - without being seen.
So the next time you go – the polar bear is pink,
And the penguins are all bright green!

So that is Mr Cranky Pants –
A man so mean and grim.
And now I've written this poem –
I'm starting to think...
Why am I friends with him??

THE ZOO

I went to the zoo – I'd not been for ages,
I wanted to see – animals in their cages.

First to the lions – coz I thought that I should,
But when I looked in – they were all
made of wood.

Then on to the rhinos – and I could have sworn,
They were paper-mache – with a big
cardboard horn.

I thought this was strange – but I
knew things were drastic,
When I peered in the pool – and the
penguins were plastic.

Even the monkeys were hideously dull.
Well they would be – they were knitted,
stuffed with cotton wool.

So I found a zoo-keeper – and asked, "Tell me what,
You've done with the real animals you've got!"

139

He replied, "I'm afraid – there aren't any about,
The Human Race has gone and wiped 'em all out."

He stared in my eyes – he didn't even blink,
"There's no creatures left son –
we've made 'em extinct!"

"I know what you're thinking – I know,
it's a shame,
But we really only have ourselves to blame…"

"Well!" I thought – "That's ruined my day!
No crocodiles swimming – no polar bears at play."

"I didn't realise that things were as
bad as all that!"
So I left the zoo and went home – to stroke
my robot cat.

MY GRANNY IS A WEREWOLF

There's something I have to warn you about.
I don't want to make you cry,
But I think my Granny's a werewolf!
I'll try and tell you why…

My suspicions started late one night
(And please try not to laugh)
I accidentally caught a glimpse
Of her getting out of the bath…

I couldn't believe my little eyes!
I didn't know what to do!
She's always had quite hairy legs,
But the rest was hairy too!

And she usually has trouble walking,
But I've noticed, on a full moon,
She'll scamper about on all fours
And chase her tail round the living room!

143

Then – when she's walking back from Bingo,
She'll give the whole street a fright!
By suddenly dropping her handbag
And howling into the night!

She used to love eating chocolate
Or humbugs would be sucked.
Now she sits watching EastEnders
Chewing pork chops that aren't cooked!

Yep – I'm sure my Granny's a werewolf!
I know – it beggars belief!
I've never seen a werewolf before,
With its own set of false teeth!

So beware of werewolves out there in the night,
And I will do the same.
Most of all, look out for the one with grey fur
Running round with a Zimmer Frame!

THE INVISIBLE MAN

I'm trying to write this poem,
On a rainy afternoon,
But I've been interrupted by The Invisible Man,
Who has just entered the room.

How do I know? Am I psychic?
Do I have special powers in my head?
Nah! He just must have gone out for
dinner last night,
His breath stinks of garlic bread…

145

THE INVISIBLE MAN II

So here I am this fine morning,
Trying to write another poem for you.
But that ruddy Invisible Man is back,
And he's putting me off again too.

How am I certain he's here again?
Do I see what no one else sees?
No – He can't have changed his socks for days
And they smell like mouldy cheese...

THE INVISIBLE MAN III

He's returned, he has, I know it!
I can't take this anymore!
Who do I mean? THE INVISIBLE MAN!
He's just crept in the door…

Why am I so certain?
Do I have some super power?
Nope – he's been jogging and reeks of sweat,
I wish he'd just go take a shower…

THE INVISIBLE MAN IV

I've got a great idea,
For a brilliant poem to write!
But you'll never guess who's putting me off,
The Invisible Man? Yep – that's right!

I know what you're thinking! Incredible!
Do I have some super sixth sense?
'Fraid not – I think he's trodden in something,
And I'm gonna throw up from the stench...

THE INVISIBLE MAN V

This is getting ridiculous!
I'm trying to write more stuff,
But that Invisible Man is back once more,
And he's really putting me off!

"Wow, Chris – that's impressive!" you say?
"Can you tell just by watching and waiting?"
Not really – his mobile phone's going off.
I can hear it in his pocket vibrating…

- brrr!
brrr!

THE INVISIBLE MAN VI

I've got some really good poems on the go!
I can't wait for you to read these!
Oh great! The Invisible Man is back!
Won't he stop putting me off – PLEASE!!

Am I so sensitive I can feel him near?
Are my senses second to none?
No – my eyes are watering – I'm gasping for air,
He's put too much aftershave on...

THE INVISIBLE MAN VII

Once more I sit here pen in hand.
Once more, my thoughts go astray.
The Invisible Man is watching me.
Why won't he just go away?

"That's awesome!" you say, "How can you tell,
The Invisible Man was coming?"
He must have heard a catchy song on the radio,
He's stood in the corner humming…

MY KITTEN

I bought myself a kitten,
It's really, really nice.
But I didn't have much money,
So the pet shop halved the price.

But as well as slashing 50%,
Off the money they had,
They also halved my kitten.
Which, at the time, I thought, quite bad.

But it doesn't seem to bother him.
And he still looks pretty sweet.
He just hasn't got a tail or a bum,
And he's only got two feet.

I've called my kitten 'Arfur.'
Coz 'Arfur Kitten' is quite funny.
I'll go back and buy the rest of him,
When I've managed to save up some money.

RECIPE FOR DISASTER

Here's my little recipe,
That everyone can make.
Listen and I'll tell you,
How to make my 'Special' Cake.

First, get you ingredients,
Some flour – that would be good.
But not just flour on its own,
No…add a little mud.

Then perhaps a couple of eggs,
Yep – that never fails.
Along with a special ingredient,
Clippings of toe nails!

Take a pinch of sugar and salt.
And sprinkle them in with care,
Not forgetting the next important bit,
A big ball of cat hair.

Maybe add some cinnamon,
Be careful – just a smidgeon.
You have to leave a little room,
For the droppings from a pigeon.

Splat your mixture into a bowl,
Your cake is nearly made!
Just stir it all up, really quickly,
With a dirty spade.

If the cake mix is too sticky,
Don't get in a muddle.
Add water, but not from the tap,
No – water from a puddle!

Now pop your cake in the oven,
And bake it up a treat!
You'll know when it is nearly done,
It'll smell like sweaty feet.

Then to make the scrumptious icing,
Use icing sugar and water I suppose.
But to add some flavour, you can add,
Whatever you find up your nose!

Spread the icing on your cake,
Then wait 'til it will harden,
And garnish with a juicy slug,
Found in your back garden.

Then pop your cake on a fancy plate,
Sprinkle with essence of blister.
And serve it up with a smile on your face,
To your brother or sister…

EDDY THE DOG

I don't need to spell it out for you,
As I'm sure you're not round the bend.
But it has to be said – my dog has two heads,
One at either end.

I've never seen anything like him before.
He's a very friendly dog though!
And it's really funny – if you tickle his tummy,
He barks in stereo!

Sure – he costs a lot to look after.
He's hungry all the time.
As he eats twice as much - dog food and such,
As any normal canine.

Some other dog owners laugh at him,
"He's useless!" I hear them talk.
But if I pop a lead in one of Eddy's mouths,
He can take himself for a walk!

But he does get himself in such a state,

If a stick for him you are throwing,

Yep – He's a great pet of mine – but most
of the time,

He doesn't know if he's coming or going....

KORKY THE CLOWN

It was Korky's first day at his clown job.
He'd wanted this job for a while.
He wanted to make people happy!
He wanted to make people smile!

Y'see, Ollie the Old Clown had retired recently,
And Korky was the next in line.
His first engagement was a
children's birthday party.
This was Korky's chance to shine!

But the kids were used to Ollie – not Korky,
They didn't think this new clown was brill…
Yep – it turns out Ollie the Old Clown,
Had left big shoes to fill…

"The Happy Ferret Family"

BLIND FERRET JOHNSON

Let me tell you the tale of a ferret I knew.
He had a wife and kids – I think there were two.
They lived in a hutch – one happy throng.
But slowly his life would go quite wrong…

HIS NAME IS FERRET JOHNSON –
the nicest creature you could meet.
HIS NAME IS FERRET JOHNSON -
his life is sweet.

Then one day his smile turned to a frown.
That ferret's life – it turned upside down.
Because when he returned to his
hutch sweet hutch.
His wife had took the kids – and not
left him much.

HIS NAME IS FERRET JOHNSON –
his wife and kids are gone.
HIS NAME IS FERRET JOHNSON –
his life's gone wrong.

Ferret Johnson collapsed in despair.
She'd not left him a table – not left him a chair.
But she'd left his guitar – so he didn't curse.
Which is good – because things are
gonna get worse….

HIS NAME IS FERRET JOHNSON –
how bad can things get?
HIS NAME IS FERRET JOHNSON –
you aint heard nothin' yet….

So the ferret sat and played guitar.

His blues songs could be heard afar.

But during a song – it came to pass.

The ferret stopped playing – he could smell gas….

HIS NAME IS FERRET JOHNSON –

his life is dire.

HIS NAME IS FERRET JOHNSON –

his home's on fire.

"Stop taking photos… RUN!!"

There were flames all around –
he flew out the door.
With the clothes he had on and guitar in his paw.
But in the explosion – he lost an eye.
But count his lucky ferrets – he didn't die.

HE'S ONE-EYED FERRET JOHNSON –
waving his hutch goodbye.
HE'S ONE EYED FERRET JOHNSON –

"ouch!"

no wife – no home – no left eye…
So he slung his guitar over his back.
And headed for the bar at the end of the track.
When he got there – he played the blues
don't you know?
But it didn't go down so well as the crowd there
preferred happy hardcore or free form jazz or disco.

HE'S ONE EYED FERRET JOHNSON –
a gang of rabbits heckled him.
HE'S ONE EYED FERRET JOHNSON –
his chances are quite slim.

The rowdy rabbits didn't like his playing.
They beat that poor ferret 'til the
room was swaying.
Fur was flying everywhere.

167

As Ferret's one good eye – shot through the air….
HE'S BLIND FERRET JOHNSON –
in a bar room brawl.
HE'S BLIND FERRET JOHNSON –
can't see at all.

He staggered outside - having lost the fight.
But worse than that – he'd lost his sight.
But he still had his guitar – slung on his back.
But he didn't see that truck speeding
down the track….

HE'S BLIND FERRET JOHNSON –
flew over the fence.
HE'S BLIND FERRET JOHNSON –
someone call an ambulance.

Then weeks went by and he couldn't be found.
When one summers evening – what was
that sound?
The finest blues songs you ever heard.
And that blind ferret singing every word!

The creatures flocked from miles away.
They all wanted to hear that ferret play.
He may be blind and his luck's been lean.
But he's the finest blues-playing ferret – you've
EVER seen!

HE'S BLIND FERRET JOHNSON –
he was born to lose.
HE'S BLIND FERRET JOHNSON –
he sings the blues.
I SAID! HE'S BLIND FERRET JOHNSON –
finally with some merit!
OH YES! HE'S BLIND FERRET JOHNSON –
the world's best, blues playing, blind,
furry ferret!!!